Taking Action

Support for Families of Adolescents with Illegal Sexual Behavior

BARBARA L. BONNER, Ph.D.

Safer Society
PRESS

BRANDON, VERMONT

Publication made possible by a generous grant from the Florence V. Burden Foundation.

ISBN: 978-1-884444-81-4

Printed in the United States of America

P.O. Box 340
Brandon, VT 05733
www.safersociety.org
(802) 247-3132

Safer Society Press is a program of the Safer Society Foundation, a 501(C)3 nonprofit dedicated to the prevention and treatment of sexual abuse. For more information, visit our Web site at www.safersociety.org.

Taking Action: Support for Families of Adolescents with Illegal Sexual Behavior

For purchasing information, including available bulk discounts, visit www.safersociety.org/press
Order # WP137

DEDICATION AND ACKNOWLEDGMENTS

I would like to dedicate this booklet to the adolescents and their deeply committed parents and caregivers who have worked with us over the past 20 years. We have learned together how to best help their children and families through a difficult time. You have our respect and admiration for standing beside your children and supporting them when they needed it the most.

I would like to acknowledge the contributions of Judith Becker, C. Eugene Walker, Mark Chaffin, Lisa Swisher, Keri Pierce, Susan Schmidt, and Dolores Subia Bigfoot to the development of our program and this booklet. My sincere appreciation goes to those who served as reviewers and the Safer Society Editors, Gaen Murphree and Marjorie Ryerson.

CONTENTS

PUBLISHER'S NOTE

This guidebook is written for you—parents and caregivers whose son or daughter has sexually offended. The moments following this discovery can be very distressing and confusing.

At this point, and over the next several months, the most important thing you can do is help your child as he or she faces the legal system and the challenge of developing new, healthier behaviors. That's where *Taking Action* comes in. Written by one of the leading authorities in the field, this guidebook provides the information you will need to support your child and access the resources you and your child will require in the days to come.

Preparation and publication of *Taking Action: Support for Families of Adolescents with Illegal Sexual Behavior* was funded by the Florence V. Burden Foundation. We are indebted to them for their support of this book and their recognition that early intervention in the troubling behaviors of children and adolescents is one of the best ways to prevent problems in adulthood and to create a safer society.

The Safer Society Foundation, Inc., is a private, nonprofit agency with a 30-year history of working to end sexual abuse and its harmful effects on families and our society. To learn more about Safer Society visit our Web site at www.safersociety.org.

You're probably reading this booklet because your son or daughter has been involved in illegal sexual behavior with another person, most likely a child, possibly even a brother or sister. If you're like most families who have been through this, you're in crisis. This could be one of the most difficult times in your whole life. You're probably wondering how to help your son or daughter, how to work with law enforcement and other systems or agencies, and how to get your life going in a better direction. You may be angry, ashamed, confused, upset, or completely stunned.

The first thing to know is that you're not alone. Other families have been in your shoes. Other families have faced this situation and come out better and stronger afterward. What's more, with the right help, most teens will successfully complete treatment and probation and go on to live healthy, constructive lives.

Let's start with the basics. What do we mean by "adolescents with illegal sexual behavior"? A general definition is a boy or girl, from ages 13 to 18, who commits an illegal sexual act as defined by the sex-crime statutes in the state or jurisdiction where the offense occurred. The laws in each state define illegal sexual acts and the ages for which these acts are considered to be illegal. Some states may include younger boys and girls in this definition. This booklet focuses primarily on adolescents who have sexually abused younger children. But adolescents are sometimes also involved in illegal sexual behavior with peers or adults, as well as behavior such as sexually explicit phone calls, publicly exposing oneself, accessing pornography on the Internet, or secretly looking at people for sexual excitement (voyeurism). This booklet does not address the illegal sexual behavior of prostitution. Sexual behavior problems occur in all kinds of families. Following are three examples of families in which adolescents have committed illegal sexual acts.

Three Case Examples

Carla Simpson was a single parent with three children. Allison was 14, Lisa was 9, and Sarah was 7. Ms. Simpson divorced the children's father three years ago, and he had regular visitation rights since then. Mr. Simpson remarried a year ago to a woman who had a son, Brandon, age 4. On a weekend visit at Mr. Simpson's house, Allison was found with Brandon in a bedroom with the door closed. When Mr. Simpson and Brandon's mother walked in, Brandon was touching Allison's vagina with his hand. The Simpsons were stunned and immediately called Ms. Simpson and told her to come pick up Allison. When questioned, Allison and Brandon stated that Allison had asked Brandon to touch her vagina but that no force was used. Brandon reported that this had happened "lots of times" when Allison visited the home. Child Protective Services (CPS) and the police investigated and Allison moved to live with her maternal grandmother. She was later adjudicated as a delinquent and referred for outpatient treatment. Over the course of treatment, she had supervised visits in her father's home with Brandon present. Allison successfully completed treatment and returned home.

Bob and LaToya Brown were the parents of Dejuan, age 16, and LaTisha, age 7. They were a middle-class family, and both children were good students and participated in school activities. Following a safety program at school, LaTisha asked to talk to her mother by herself. She started crying and told her mother that a friend of Dejuan's, Troy, age 16, had asked her to "do it" and she had let him; he had put his penis in her vagina. She said it had happened twice in Dejuan's bedroom when Troy was staying overnight and Dejuan was sleeping in the living room. LaTisha's parents took LaTisha to a nearby hospital where she was examined and interviewed by a physician and a hospital social worker. The social worker contacted the local police and child welfare services to report the incident. When confronted by the police, Troy admitted what he had done and said that he knew it was wrong when he did it. Troy was placed in detention and his parents obtained an attorney to represent him. He was later adjudicated as a delinquent and court-ordered into treatment. He completed treatment and no additional problematic sexual behavior was reported.

Rosa Rojas was a single parent who had four children by two different fathers. Manual, the oldest, was 15, and often took the role of the man of the house. He had been on probation a year earlier for breaking and entering a neighbor's apartment and stealing several items. Angela, age 10, helped her mother with the younger children, Reynaldo, age 6, and Starla, age 4. Ms. Rojas worked days and weekends to support her children, and Manual or Ms. Rojas's grandmother, who lived close by, often supervised them. One day, a neighbor called Ms. Rojas to report that her two children, a 6-year-old boy and a 5-year-old girl, had been playing at the Rojas's home the day before. The grandmother and Manual were supervising the children. The neighbor said that while the grandmother was taking a nap, Manual had the neighbor's children and his two younger siblings play "Truth or Dare" with him. The children reported that the game involved sexual interactions between all of the children and Manual, including oral sex and digital penetration. They also stated that Manual had threatened to get them into trouble if they didn't play the "game." The neighbor was upset and angry and had already called the police. Law enforcement then placed Manual in detention and conducted an investigation. The investigation revealed that Manual had committed illegal sexual acts with his younger siblings over several months. The court determined that he was delinquent and placed him in a secure setting for treatment. After nine months in the facility, Manual moved to a foster home. He later returned to his home and high school with no further sexual behavior problems.

We've written this booklet to help you get through the difficult situation in which you find yourself, and to make the best choices for your son or daughter and for your whole family. We want to give you the best information currently available about the things you need to know right now. This includes

- why teens sexually abuse others;
- how to stay calm and take action;
- how to find a good treatment program;
- how to work with the legal system, Child Protective Services (CPS), and other agencies;
- how or if to talk to your teen's school, and your friends, family, and neighbors about what happened;
- how to prevent your teen from becoming involved in future illegal sexual behavior;

- how to protect siblings and the family as a whole; and
- how to best help your son or daughter.

We've tried to discuss the issues that are the most important to parents as they face this situation. We've also suggested some places where you can get more answers and information.

Throughout this booklet, we address ourselves to "parents." But we know that you might just as easily be an aunt, grandparent, or other extended family member, a close friend of the family, a foster parent, or some other caregiver. We also talk mostly about boys because boys commit about 90 percent of all illegal sexual behaviors by youth under the age of 18. But we know that teenage girls can be involved in illegal or harmful sexual behavior, too. We also know that while most teens sexually abuse younger kids, adolescents commit illegal sexual acts against other adolescents or sometimes with adults. So if you're a caregiver who is not the teen's parent, or if your teen with illegal sexual behavior is a girl, or if your teen's illegal sexual behavior isn't exactly described here, please keep reading. Everyone's situation is different. Take from this booklet what is helpful to you and your family.

We wrote this booklet to help you and your family as you work through your teen's problem and the challenges of your current situation. Having a child involved in the legal or child protection system is difficult. Learning that your teen has harmed another person, especially another child, can be particularly difficult. But we know that adolescents can change and that families can grow stronger as a result of working through problems. We know this firsthand. At the Center on Child Abuse and Neglect, we've provided treatment to boys and girls and their families and conducted research on adolescents with illegal sexual behavior for over 20 years. In that time, we've seen hundreds of teens accept responsibility and change. We've seen families learn and grow. We've seen adolescents and families who had given up on each other find strength and hope and better lives, and so can your family.

ONE

Facing a Family Crisis

What Do I Do Now?

Most parents have a very strong negative response when they first learn that their teen has sexually harmed a child. Many consider it the worst moment of their lives. Parents tell us they feel shocked, furious, disappointed, and confused. They find it hard to believe that their son or daughter could do such a thing. They don't know which way to turn, whom to call or trust, or what to do. Most have never had to deal with the police, Child Protective Services, or the legal system. They blame themselves, their teen, sometimes even the victim. Faced with the news, parents scream, yell, cry, threaten—and sometimes resort to threats or blows. These responses are understandable, but they rarely help. There is nothing you can do to change the past but there are a number of things that you can do to help your family and your child.

What Should I Do Instead?

Most parents can't possibly be calm and helpful when they first learn about their teen's harmful sexual behavior. As with any crisis situation with a teenager, it's best first to separate yourself from your child, calm yourself down, and try to think clearly about what needs to be done. Once you feel more calm and collected, however, your adolescent needs to know that

- you still love him, despite the sexually harmful behavior;

- he must tell the truth about what he did;
- he must take responsibility for his behavior; and
- you will support him during treatment.

It's okay to let him know that you are upset, disappointed, and angry about what he did, but he also needs to know that you will stand with him and do what is necessary to get help. It's okay for your son to realize that he has disappointed you, that he has let his family and others down, and that he will have to work hard to regain your trust.

Then What?

You need to make some decisions, and you need to make them thoughtfully and carefully. The following concerns are usually the most important to address first:

1. Is the child victim safe? Are there other children that need protection? What needs to be done to make certain that there is no contact between the teen and the child or other possible victims?
2. Is your teen safe? Will he try to hurt himself or run away now that his behavior has been discovered?
3. Do you need to call the police or Child Protective Services and report the behavior?
4. Do you need to call an attorney or a public defender to answer your questions?
5. Should you call other family members, friends, or clergy to help you deal with the situation and make decisions more effectively?

These questions can be difficult to answer, so most parents do find it helpful to involve a trusted relative, friend, or clergy member for support and help with making these decisions. It is important to consider each decision carefully because each one can have significant consequences for your son or daughter and for your family as you move ahead.

Was It My Fault?

Parents often look back and think, "I should have seen that coming"; "I should have been suspicious"; or "How could I not have known that this was happening?" But only in rare cases do parents have clues that their son or daughter might sexually abuse another person. The signs of problematic sexual behavior are hard to recognize because teens hide their sexual behavior from adults, and especially from their parents. In most cases, parents had no way to know that they should have intervened.

Telling Others about Your Adolescent's Illegal Sexual Behavior

It can be difficult to decide what—or if—to tell other people about your son's or daughter's behavior. Do you tell grandparents, other family members, school personnel, or friends? Whom do you tell? And what do you tell them? Some issues are discussed below to help you think through these decisions.

Who Needs to Know?

If your adolescent is living at home and others will be supervising him, they need to know that he needs close supervision. This is to reduce any possible problematic behavior, to eliminate the chance of his behavior with a child being misinterpreted, and to provide maximum protection for children. While they may not need to know exactly what happened, they need to be given basic information, such as, "Jerry made a mistake and the court has put him on probation. He needs to have an adult supervise him at all times, so he needs to be where you can see him and what he's doing."

If the person asks what he did, you can say, "Our lawyer said it was best not to discuss it"; or "We have decided to keep it just between Jerry and us"; or "It was an instance of bad judgment and he is in treatment (or on probation). By the way, he's doing very well and we are proud of his progress."

It may, however, be necessary to tell other family members, particularly if your son or daughter will be living with them. It is recommended that you discuss what you will say with your teen so that he will know what has been said. In most cases, a detailed account is not necessary. It does need to be clear, however, that the teen needs rules in the home, supervision, and that the requirements of probation must be met.

In some states, probation officers are required to notify school personnel if a youth has been adjudicated as a delinquent, typically for a serious behavior. Depending on the school system, the teen may be allowed to continue classes, to be suspended, expelled, or assigned to an alternative school setting. If the state does not require that this information be provided to the school, parents may or may not decide to inform school personnel about their son's behavior or probation plan. It is recommended that parents discuss this issue with their teen's attorney and treatment provider before they make a decision.

In general, the rule about whom to tell should be, Do they need to know? If not, the information does not need to be discussed.

Taking Care of Yourself

Putting your life back together after your child has been involved in illegal sexual behavior is highly stressful for all members of the family. As a parent, it is particularly stressful. So it is important that you remember to plan some things to increase your positive feelings and outlook. Some activities that may help you cope with the stress include

- taking an active part in your adolescent's treatment program;
- taking a walk every day with family members;
- talking with trusted friends or family members who can give you reassurance and support;
- planning and doing fun things together as a family;
- using some relaxation exercises every day; and
- thinking positive thoughts about the future.

It is important to remember that most teens with illegal sexual behavior respond well to treatment and are not involved in any further illegal sexual behavior. Even though at this time it may feel like this incident is a horrible disaster from which your family will never recover, keep your thoughts on the positive aspects in this booklet and know that the chances are good that your teen and your family will recover.

TWO

Understanding Adolescents with Illegal Sexual Behavior

Why Did This Happen?

Most parents want to know why this happened. Why did their teen sexually harm someone else? But it's often difficult, if not impossible, to determine exactly why. There is almost never a single reason why a teen engages in illegal sexual behavior. More often such behavior is the result of many factors. Following are the most common reasons.

Curiosity / Experimentation

Most adolescents are curious about sex. Some of them will take advantage of an opportunity to find out more—with younger children. They know it's wrong. They know they shouldn't do it. They know they'll get in trouble if they get caught. What they usually don't know is that the police may come to their school and take them into custody and that they may be held in detention and charged as a delinquent, or in some cases, with an adult crime.

Impulsivity / Immaturity

Research tells us that all teenage boys are immature and impulsive to some degree. But some teenagers are more immature and more impulsive than others. Some may be diagnosed with Attention-Deficit Hyperactivity Disorder (ADHD) and have poor judgment about relationships and actions. The ADHD does not "cause" the harmful sexual behavior, but it can be related to impulsive behavior and poor decision-making skills. (It is important to note that most youth with ADHD do not have problematic sexual behavior.)

Delinquency / Aggression

Some teens have a history of delinquent behavior and repeatedly engage in aggressive acts toward others. Their illegal sexual behavior is one more aggressive act in a series of illegal and aggressive behaviors.

Psychological Problems

Some boys who commit illegal sexual acts have serious psychological problems, such as depression or Post-Traumatic Stress Disorder. The mental illness itself does not "cause" the illegal sexual behavior but it may affect their feelings, judgments, and choices. They may be isolated and feel left out of normal teen activities and turn to children as substitutes for age-appropriate relationships.

Exposure to Sexual Materials or Behaviors

Teenagers today have easy access to highly sexualized materials through movies, television, music, the Internet, and magazines. Sex is used to sell almost everything, and ordinary media content is more highly sexualized than ever. Some boys report that they were viewing sexually explicit materials prior to their illegal behavior and that this material influenced their actions. Some teens live in a highly sexualized home with frequent, open sexual behavior between adults. This environment, too, can affect their choices and behaviors.

Sexual Abuse

Some adolescents have themselves been sexually abused. The abuse might have been recent, might be ongoing, or could be something that happened when they were much younger. The majority of teens with illegal sexual behavior, however, have not been sexually abused.

Problems with Sexual Attraction to Children

A small number of adolescents may be sexually attracted to children rather than to age-appropriate peers. They may be developing a mental disorder known as pedophilia. Pedophilia involves intense sexual arousal to children 13 or younger. To be diagnosed, the person must be at least 16 years old and at least five years older than the child. This is a rare condition in adolescents and only a qualified professional should make a diagnosis.

What we know is that your son may have been involved in illegal sexual behavior for many reasons. Each boy's reasons are different. Each family is different. What's important now is to understand which of these factors are most relevant for your son. Then you and your son's treatment provider can work together to get him going in the right direction again so that he can have a safe and productive future.

Understanding teens with illegal sexual behavior is a complex challenge. Even the experts who provide treatment according to the best available evidence know that they are working with just that, the best evidence currently available. Our knowledge of adolescents who engage in illegal sexual behavior is constantly changing and expanding.

One important thing to know is that youth under age 18 commit a substantial number of the sex offenses committed in the United States. At least one-third of all sexual abuse of children is committed by boys and girls under 18. And according to the U.S. Department of Justice, adolescents account for about 17 percent of all arrests for sex offenses. Boys commit the majority of these offenses, an estimated 90 percent, and girls commit about 10 percent of the offenses.

Questions Most Commonly Asked by Parents

Most parents have unanswered questions about teens who engage in illegal sexual behavior. Most parents must sort through a lot of wrong information as they try to get a better understanding of their son's or daughter's behavior. What follows are answers to questions most commonly asked by parents, based on the best and most reliable information we have now. Because teenage boys and girls with illegal sexual behavior have some differences, we'll discuss each gender separately.

Q. Do these boys go on to become adult sex offenders?
A. Current research shows that the majority of adolescents with illegal sexual behavior do not go on to become adult sex offenders. Moreover, if a boy with illegal sexual behavior receives treatment, he is far less likely to reoffend. Research shows that the sexual reoffense rate for adolescents who receive treatment is low, from 3 to 14 percent. The idea that a major-

ity of adolescents will become adult sex offenders is not supported by the research done over the past 20 years.

Q. What kinds of families do boys with illegal sexual behavior have?
A. We have seen all types of families. The families of boys with illegal sexual behavior are as different as the boys themselves. Some are well-functioning families and have one or both biological parents in the home. Others families include step-parents or grandparents, foster or adoptive parents, or kinship parents. The families have many different levels of income and education, and they represent all ethnicities. Many of these families would be considered normal families, with only typical family problems. Other families include high levels of stress along with a history of problems with maltreatment, substance abuse, domestic violence, and/or unstable employment.

Q. What type of boy commits this behavior?
A. All types of boys commit illegal sexual behavior, including

- boys with no previous delinquent behavior to boys with an extensive history of aggressive or delinquent acts;
- boys with no major behavior problems at home or school to boys with significant problems at home and in school;
- boys with good school performance and grades to boys with poor school performance and learning problems;
- boys with no history of abuse, neglect, or serious family problems to boys with a history of abuse or neglect and highly problematic family situations;
- boys with good social skills and friendships to boys with poor social skills and few or no friends; and
- boys with positive peer group and school activities to boys with a delinquent peer group and low involvement in school activities.

Q. Do adolescents commit serious sex offenses?
A. Some do. While some teens' sexually harmful behavior is limited to touching a child or having a child touch them, others have extensive, aggressive sexual behavior that includes forced vaginal or anal penetration.

Q. Were these boys sexually abused as children?
A. Some were; many were not. Anywhere from 20 to 50 percent of teenage boys with illegal sexual behavior report being sexually abused as children. Several studies have shown that previous physical and/or psychological abuse or neglect may also play an important role. But many of these boys have not experienced any past maltreatment.

Q. Do boys tell the truth about what they did?
A. Some boys immediately admit the illegal sexual behavior when questioned by their parents or the parents of the victim. Others admit the behavior when questioned by the police or Child Protective Services. Others admit much later, after they enter treatment. Some boys say they did not do anything, and they stick to that story for months. These boys often refuse to admit the truth because they are afraid of the consequences. Such boys report that the longer they don't tell the truth, the harder it is to tell the truth later.

Q. Do these boys have other psychological problems?
A. Some do; many do not. Some have learning disabilities or Attention-Deficit Hyperactivity Disorder (ADHD). Others have more serious problems, including depression or Post-Traumatic Stress Disorder (PTSD), both of which need to be addressed during treatment.

Q. Are these adolescents similar to adult sex offenders?
A. No. Most adolescents with illegal sexual behavior are quite different from adult sex offenders. Adolescents engage in fewer illegal acts over shorter periods of time, their behavior is less aggressive, and most importantly, their rate of future illegal sexual behavior is lower than adult sex offenders.

Q. Who are the victims?

A. Most teenage boys have sexual activity with younger children that they know and spend time with. This includes younger siblings, cousins, children of a neighbor, or children that they babysit. It is unusual for an adolescent boy to have illegal sexual behavior with a child he doesn't know. Adolescents rarely abuse children they see on a playground or in a mall; this behavior is more likely to be committed by an adult sex offender.

Q. If my son abused a young boy, does that mean he's gay?

A. Adolescents are involved with both young boys and girls. They typically do not prefer one gender over the other. They are involved with whichever age or gender child they are around and can get to participate. If an adolescent is involved with young boys, this does not mean he's homosexual or will become a homosexual as an adult. It typically means that he has access to a young boy and has gotten him to participate in sexual activity. It may mean that he's more comfortable experimenting sexually with boys than with girls. It is not a definite indicator of homosexuality.

In rare instances, an adolescent boy will just be sexually attracted to young boys. While there is no long-term information on these boys, the behavior might indicate a longer-term interest in young boys, i.e., pedophilia. If an adolescent has signs of developing pedophilia, this issue should be directly addressed in treatment.

Q. Do these adolescents commit other illegal or delinquent acts?

A. Yes, many do. The rate of future delinquent behavior in these teens, such as shoplifting, using illegal drugs, or possessing stolen property, is significantly higher than the rate of future illegal sexual behavior. Parents need to be aware of the risk for other possible delinquent behavior with these teens and provide close supervision of their friends and activities.

Q. Should adolescents be allowed to have a cell phone during this process?

A. The use of a cell phone should be decided based on whether the adolescent needs a phone. For example, how often is a phone necessary to check on a ride home, contact parents at work, check in with parents, etc.? Parents may be concerned that the phone is used inappropriately, i.e., sending sexual messages or accessing sexual information. Parents should carefully monitor the use of a phone and remove it immediately if they have any concerns about how the adolescent is using it.

Q. What kind of financial costs are involved?
A. There can be costs for legal services and for treatment. In some cases, parents hire a private attorney and pay for the adolescent's treatment. In other cases, the state will appoint an attorney to represent the adolescent at no cost to the family and the county or state will pay for the treatment program. In these cases, there is no cost for the legal and treatment services.

However, there can be other costs involved. There are costs for gas to and from treatment and time off work to participate in the treatment program. These costs need to be considered as they can add stress to the family.

Q. Can the family of the victim personally sue me or my son or daughter?
A. This is an important question that should be discussed with an attorney.

Adolescent Girls with Illegal Sexual Behavior

At present, researchers have limited information on adolescent girls with illegal sexual behavior toward children. This lack of information is due to a number of reasons. Girls' sexually abusive behavior is considered to be underreported to law enforcement and Child Protective Services. Also, most of the research has been based on small numbers of girls. As such, the research may not accurately represent this group as a whole. Here are some of the important aspects of what we know now:

- Adolescent girls commit a range of illegal sexual behaviors, ranging from limited behaviors based on curiosity to repeated, aggressive acts.
- The most common sexual offenses by adolescent girls are nonaggressive acts, such as mutual fondling, that occur in an activity such as babysitting.

- Adolescent girls account for about 10 percent of all arrests for sexual offenses by youth under age 18 and 1 percent of forcible rapes.
- The most frequent victims are 5-year-old children who are acquaintances or relatives of the teen.
- Most adolescent girls are well-functioning with limited behavioral problems while some have severe behavioral, psychiatric, or delinquent histories.
- Compared to boys, most adolescent girls with illegal sexual behavior have a more extensive and severe history of physical and sexual abuse. The girls were abused at younger ages than boys and were more likely to have been abused by multiple perpetrators.
- The rate of future sexual offenses by adolescent girls is not known.

THREE

Understanding the Legal System and Child Protective Services

Several stages exist for possible legal and Child Protective Services (CPS) involvement for adolescents with illegal sexual behavior. The stages are described here in general, but it should be noted that the procedures followed differ depending on the laws and policies in each state. In some states, the counties determine whether or not CPS is involved in these cases.

We know it can be difficult for you to deal with the legal system and CPS under any circumstances. It is even more difficult when your child has been involved in illegal sexual behavior. It can seem like people outside your family are making all the decisions about what your family has to do and what will happen to your child. You may think the decisions are unnecessary, unfair, and not the best thing for your child or your family.

It is important to remember that the legal system exists to protect the community. Police officers, state attorneys, probation officers, and judges are required to take certain steps to make sure that people are safe. In juvenile court, those key judicial people are required to establish a plan so that children such as yours will not have illegal behavior in the future. As the parents of an offending teenager, you should use your son's attorney to help you effectively deal with the legal system. A private attorney or public defender can provide you with information and advice that will be extremely helpful in dealing with the legal issues involved, such as how your son should respond to the charges, how a plea agreement can be made, and what rules the boy will need to follow while on probation.

In many cases, your family will be involved with Child Protective Services (CPS), the state agency that works with families to protect children from abuse and neglect. CPS is usually involved if the victim is in your home or if you have young children who might be at risk. CPS's role is to make certain that all children in your family are safe. CPS typically recommends that the adolescent be removed from the home for a period of time. Depending on both the offending youth's progress in treatment and the family's situation, CPS may later recommend that the youth be reunified with his family or that he not be returned to the home.

CPS personnel are often directly involved with the family, spend time in the home, and make recommendations that affect the whole family. Parents frequently complain that this process is intrusive to their family and not necessary for the protection of their children. It is often difficult for a family to have such a close inspection of its personal activities, and parents can easily become upset and frustrated from the process. As with legal personnel, it is important to remember that CPS staff have a required job to do, even though, at times, the staff's role can be difficult for your family to accept.

It will be helpful if you understand the roles of the legal and child protection system and make every effort to work with personnel in those systems to make the process as manageable as possible. If you understand what legal and CPS personnel are doing and why they are doing it, things will go more smoothly. It is important for you to be cooperative, have patience, and know as much as possible about the legal system and CPS.

Steps in the System, From Investigation through Case Closed

Step 1: Investigation

After a report of illegal sexual behavior has been made to CPS or the police, the first step is to conduct an investigation of the report to determine if the behavior occurred. The investigation is typically conducted by law enforcement and/or CPS personnel. Law enforcement's role is to determine if a delinquent or illegal act was committed. If the behavior was reported to have occurred to another child within your family, CPS will be involved to determine the safety of that child and any other children in the home.

Depending on their ages and language abilities, the children involved will typically be interviewed by police or CPS to obtain information about what happened. You, your son, members of your family, or other individuals will be interviewed in order to provide a thorough investigation.

Your son may be taken to a police station and interviewed by law enforcement officers. Most states require that you or another adult be present when your son is interviewed and that the Miranda rights (the right to remain silent and the right to an attorney) are read and understood. Your family may choose to have an attorney present at the interview to represent your teen. You also have the right not to participate in an interview.

If the information obtained in the investigation indicates that illegal sexual behavior occurred, police will forward the information to a state's attorney who will determine if charges are to be filed against the adolescent. CPS personnel will make recommendations to the court about steps to be taken to ensure the safety of all other children in your home.

Step 2: Charges Filed

If the state's attorney determines that it is appropriate to file charges, the charges can be filed against an adolescent in juvenile court, for what is termed a delinquent act, or in adult court, as a criminal act. The decision about whether the charges will be filed in juvenile or adult court typically depends on factors such as the adolescent's age, the seriousness of the illegal behavior, and his previous history of illegal behavior. It is important to note, however, that the objective of the juvenile system is to rehabilitate youth while the objective of the adult criminal system is to punish individuals. Both court systems are committed to providing maximum safety to the community. Most cases of illegal sexual behavior by youth under age 18 are handled by the juvenile courts in order to provide rehabilitation services to the adolescents.

Your family can hire an attorney to represent your adolescent. If you cannot afford an attorney, the court will help you obtain an attorney. You and your child, in consultation with his attorney, will then decide how he will respond to the charges—that is, whether he will offer a plea of "yes," he committed the act, or "no," he did not, or another response recommended by your attorney. If he decides to plead not guilty and have a trial, the case can be tried before a judge, or in some cases, before a jury. In most cases, the boy and his caregivers agree on how he will plead.

However, the decision to plead guilty or not guilty is made by your son in consultation with his attorney.

If charges are not filed, the case may be closed by the legal system and no further action will be taken. In these cases, Child Protective Services may remain involved and monitor a treatment plan for your family to ensure the safety of all children in the home.

Note: This process can take months to complete. Parents need to stay in contact with their son's attorney during this time.

Step 3: Court Decision

In juvenile court, if your adolescent committed the act and decides to admit it, a plea may be arranged with the state's attorney and a hearing before a judge will be held. If your son is found to have committed the illegal sexual behavior, he will be assigned to a juvenile justice agency. He may stay in the community with a probation plan or be placed outside your home in a group home or facility. If your son requests a trial and he is found not guilty, the case will be closed by the legal system.

Step 4: Probation

If your child is placed on probation and remains in the community, he will usually be assigned a probation officer who will supervise his behavior and activities. He will have a set of rules to follow, such as a curfew, regular school attendance, participation in one or more treatment programs, no contact with young children, community service, no further illegal behavior, and payment of court costs. In addition, you may be ordered to attend your son's treatment program.

The length of probation usually depends on how long it takes to complete the probation plan. The adolescent will have hearings scheduled before a judge to monitor his progress in completing the probation requirements. The probation officer and treatment provider will furnish reports of your son's progress to the court on a regular basis. If the teen violates the probation plan, the judge can order a more restrictive placement, or additional sanctions.

Step 5: Case Closed
When the probation requirements are met, your child's case will be closed. You should check with your attorney to determine if your son's records can be expunged (destroyed), as the procedures differ from state to state.

Placement

If it is determined that your son performed illegal sexual acts, the judge or the state's juvenile justice agency will decide where he will be placed. Placement can be either in your home, in another home in the community, or in a more secure setting. The placement depends on the severity of the behavior and the threat the adolescent poses to children in the home or in the community. Who makes the decision about where the teen will be placed is determined differently in different states. In some states, the juvenile justice agency makes the decision; in other states, the judge makes the decision. In most juvenile courts, the prosecuting and defense attorneys, the judge, CPS staff, and probation/juvenile justice personnel agree on the decision. It is important for you to meet with your son's attorney before a decision is made about where he will be placed. If you do not agree with the placement decision, you need to work with your son's attorney to see if changes can be made. You may be able to participate in this process, particularly if your son is to remain in the community rather than be placed in a residential setting.

Any possible negative effects of out-of-home or out-of-community placement should be considered when making placement decisions. Negative effects can include an increased risk of future illegal behavior due to his involvement with other delinquent peers, the weakening of family ties, the absence of his family's involvement in treatment, and a lack of normal adolescent social experiences.

Most professionals recommend that an adolescent who has offended against a child in his home be placed outside the home but remain in the community. Depending on the circumstances of the case, however, he may live with his family during probation and treatment. For adolescents who are allowed to live in the community, many live with another family member or an approved friend of the family. If this is the case for your adolescent, you will need to assist the probation officer or CPS personnel in finding an appropriate place for your son to live. Probation officials, the court, and/or CPS must approve your son's placement. The requirements for his supervision need to be clearly understood and agreed to by all involved adults. He will need to live where he will be well supervised and in a place where he is required to complete all aspects of his probation requirements. It is best if your teen can continue to attend his regular school and participate in ongoing school activities, but this is not always possible. Your son needs to understand that his behavior has caused many changes in his family, and the consequences of his behavior may mean that he has to change schools or not be involved in sports or other important activities that he likes.

You may want to keep your son in your own home during probation and treatment, although this is not typically done if the victim is also in the home. For this placement to be approved, Child Protective Services would have to review the procedures that are in place in the home in order to provide complete safety at all times for the victim and other children in the home.

Some adolescents need to be placed in a more restricted setting, such as a group home, a residential facility, or a secure setting for youth. Decisions about a teen's placement in a restricted setting will depend on many factors, including the type of treatment he needs, the level of supervision that is necessary, and community safety.

A small number of adolescents require psychiatric hospitalization to address their treatment needs. The hospitalization can be short- or long-term, depending on whether the purpose is to stabilize the child or to address their psychiatric problems. Some hospitals conduct treatment programs for adolescents with illegal sexual behavior as part of the youths' overall treatment plan. Youth who are hospitalized should be discharged when their mental health disorders have stabilized and they have made progress in treatment. They may be released to continue treatment in a community-based program and have ongoing monitoring of their mental health disorder.

FOUR

Understanding Treatment

Treatment Providers

Most adolescents with illegal sexual behavior are treated by profession-als from mental health disciplines, such as social work, psychology, and psychiatry. It is recommended that providers

- be licensed mental health professionals or work under the supervision of a licensed professional;
- have previous general experience working with adolescents and their families;
- be familiar with the literature regarding adolescents with illegal sexual behavior;
- participate in training and continuing education for treating youth with illegal sexual behavior; and
- be members of relevant professional organizations such as the Association for Treatment of Sexual Abusers (ATSA) and the American Professional Society on the Abuse of Children (APSAC).

Some states have special certification requirements for individuals who treat adolescents with illegal sexual behavior.

In some areas, treatment is provided by juvenile justice personnel, who are typically probation officers. These treatment providers work under the supervision of the juvenile justice system. They have received training in treating adolescents with illegal sexual behavior. The recommenda-tions we suggest above for mental health professionals, such as specialized training and knowledge of the literature, also apply to this group of treatment providers.

Approaches to Treatment

Several treatment approaches are currently being used to treat adolescents with illegal sexual behavior. Depending on the court and the availability of treatment, the judge or probation officer may recommend, or order, an adolescent to be part of a specific program or the parents may have a choice of providers. In some cases, the legal/juvenile justice system may pay for the treatment. In other cases, it will be the parents' responsibility. These are decisions that need to be discussed with your child's attorney or a representative of the court/juvenile justice system.

Parents need to have information about the various approaches to treatment and, if they have a choice of providers, must decide what would be best for their teenager. Questions for parents to consider, as they weigh this decision, are the following:

- Is the provider licensed to provide mental health services in the state, or is the provider working in an agency under supervisors who are licensed?
- Does the provider have adequate knowledge about these adolescents, i.e., does he/she know most of the information in this booklet?
- Is the provider familiar with the literature of the field? Does the provider attend annual trainings for this population and have membership in professional organizations?
- Does he/she know which approaches to treatment are the most effective and how many adolescents will have future illegal sexual behavior?

A good treatment program would be one with experienced, licensed therapists, with a good working relationship with the court, probation

staff, and CPS, and with a reputation for providing effective services to
these adolescents. A questionable program is one that utilizes therapists
with limited knowledge and experience with this population, professionals without a license, providers who see all adolescents with illegal
sexual behavior as high risk for reoffending, treatment approaches that
are questionable with adolescents (i.e., use of the polygraph), no follow-
up information on other adolescents they have treated, and/or treatment
techniques used with adults.

Several approaches have been used to treat adolescents with illegal
sexual behavior. Depending on the particular case, one or more of the
interventions described below will typically be used.

Multisystemic Therapy (MST)
Multisystemic therapy is an approach to treatment that has been highly
successful in decreasing general delinquent behavior and substance abuse
by adolescents. The treatment provider is available 24 hours a day, 7 days
a week and works closely with the youth and his parents. MST is not
about going to therapy for an hour a week, as in other approaches. In this
approach, the therapist has only a few clients and spends a lot of time with
the teen and his parents. The therapist works directly with the parents to
improve the boy's behavior and grades, his social activities, and his behavior at home. Studies show that MST is effective with adolescents with illegal sexual behavior. Treatment usually takes about four to six months and
is done in the community, as it must directly involve the caregivers.

Cognitive Behavioral Group Therapy
Cognitive Behavioral Group Therapy is a psychoeducational approach
to treatment that is conducted in groups of six to eight adolescents.
This approach addresses issues such as taking responsibility for the illegal behavior; learning legal, appropriate sexual behavior; and preventing
future illegal sexual and nonsexual behavior. Adolescents attend weekly
1- to 1½-hour group sessions in the community for 8 to 24 months,
depending on the program's requirements. This treatment approach is
widely accepted and used for adolescents. Limited research is available,
however, that compares this approach to other types of interventions to

see if it is the best one to use. An educational support group for parents is typically part of the treatment program.

Individual Therapy

Individual therapy may be provided if other forms of treatment, such as MST or group therapy, are not available or if the adolescent has other psychological problems that need to be addressed. In this approach, a therapist typically meets with the adolescent on a weekly basis for an hour to address issues related to his illegal sexual behavior. If the youth has other psychological problems, such as depression, these would also be addressed in the individual sessions. In these cases, it is recommended that the teen's caregivers be included in the treatment on a regular basis. The caregiver can provide important information on the boy's behavior at home, at school, and in the community. The therapist can discuss issues of behavior management, supervision, and progress in treatment during the sessions.

Family Therapy

Family therapy is used to directly address the illegal sexual behavior or to focus on problems within the family that influence the youth's progress in treatment. Family therapy usually involves all members of the family and may be particularly useful in cases where the sexual behavior occurred within the family. This approach can be used as the primary approach to treatment or when the family is involved in the reunification process.

Getting the Most Out of Treatment

Some treatment programs for adolescents require parental attendance and participation while others have limited parental involvement. We recommend that you actively participate in the treatment to the extent that is suggested or required by the program. It will be helpful for you to understand what your son is learning in the program, and how to provide supervision and the best support to your adolescent.

You also need to consider obtaining treatment for the child victim if the abuse occurred within the family. Depending on the extent and severity of the behavior, the child may only need an assessment and a brief intervention. In more serious cases, the child may need a more extended intervention. The adolescent's treatment provider or a CPS case worker may be able to provide names of therapists with expertise in treating child victims.

In some cases, an adolescent's illegal sexual behavior can result in problems for one or both parents, if they, too, have a personal history of abuse. It is quite difficult to deal with a child's sexual behavior when problems remain from the parents' past. In these cases, it is important for the parents to seek services to address their own problems so that they can then best help their child.

When the caregivers are involved in their son's treatment, many have positive reports at the end of treatment. They report that they communicate better with their adolescent, their family is closer than before the illegal behavior, and their teen has matured and is doing well in school and at home. These are the outcomes that providers hope will happen for all adolescents and their families.

Length of Treatment

The length of treatment varies from program to program and depends on

- the seriousness of the sexual behavior;
- whether the youth has other delinquent behavior; and
- the youth's and family's participation and progress in treatment.

Adolescents who are in community-based programs and live in the community are treated in shorter-term, less-intensive programs that usually meet once a week for one to two hours and last from 8 to 24 months. Some adolescents need long-term, intensive treatment in a restricted placement. Programs in these settings typically use a "levels system" by which the youth's progress is measured and rewarded as he moves through the levels to discharge.

FIVE

Communicating with Your Adolescent

Good communication with your teenager is one of the foundations of good parenting. It is even more important in stressful situations, such as what your family is going through. As children become adolescents, they normally get more involved with peers and talk less to parents. Less communication with parents can be a normal part of establishing independence, but teenagers still want and need to communicate with their parents, feel close to their parents, and be able to turn to their parents when they have problems or when they need to talk. Here are some tips for how to establish good communication with your teenager.

Listen

Listening is the single best thing you can do to establish good communication. Listening sounds simple, but often isn't. Let your teenager finish his thoughts. Let him tell the whole story. Remember that listening doesn't necessarily mean agreeing with everything he says. Sometimes he just needs to talk and to know that you understand. You don't have to interrupt, agree or disagree, or come up with an immediate solution to his problems. For starters, you just have to listen. Following are some simple listening rules.

Pay Attention
Try to focus on what your teen is saying, rather than thinking about what you want to say back. Stop what you are doing, if you need to, in order to pay attention. Get rid of distractions so that you can pay attention.

Repeat from Time to Time

Sometimes you can restate things your teenager has said in order to make sure you've got it right. This helps you understand, and also shows that you are listening. Be careful not to jump to conclusions when you repeat. For example, if your teenager says, "I forgot to call my probation officer yesterday. I don't know why I have to call in every week. I'm doing fine. That's a stupid rule." you could say:

Good Repeating

"So, you wonder why you have to call in when you're doing fine, right?" or "Sounds like it's hard to remember to call Mr. Johnson when you're doing okay, right?"

Poor Repeating (jumping to conclusions)

"So, you want to break the rules again, right?" or, "You know you have to call Mr. Johnson every week, so just go do it right now."

Ask Occasional Questions

Asking occasional questions shows you are listening and interested. Be careful not to ask too many questions or to take over the conversation with questions. In the example above, you might ask, "What did Mr. Johnson say when you talked to him last week?" or "What if you gave him a call today?"

Listen Nonjudgmentally

When your teenager is talking to you about a concern or a problem, try not to judge or criticize him while you are in "listening mode." Listen first. Hold your opinions until later, after your adolescent has finished.

Communicate in Specifics

Teenagers need specifics, especially when it comes to communicating about rules and expectations. When giving your teenager instructions or criticism, talk about specific behaviors, not personalities or generalities. Also, whenever possible, tell the teen what to do, rather than what not to do.

Talk About Behavior, Not Personalities

For example, if your teenager has failed to do his chores you might say, "You haven't finished your chores; I want you to get them done," instead of, "You think you're too old to do chores?" or "If you weren't so irresponsible, I wouldn't have to remind you."

Talk About Specifics, Not Generalities

For example, it's better to say, "Last week, you weren't ready to leave to go to treatment on time," instead of "You're never on time when we have to leave to go to treatment; you mess around every week."

Be Understanding

Show that you understand how your teen feels. Even if you don't necessarily agree with what your teenager is saying, it is still helpful to put yourself in his shoes and communicate to him that you understand how he feels.

Use "Door Openers" Rather Than "Door Closers" in Communicating

Door Openers

"Tell me what happened."
"What do you think is the right thing to do?"
"How do you feel about that?"
"What happened next?"
"That's a good question."

Door Closers

"I'll tell you what you ought to do…"
"I don't want to hear that kind of talk."
"So what?"
"Why are you asking me?"
"Don't come crying to me if you end up in a mess."

Take Time Out When Things Get Heated

Parent–teenager arguments are a normal part of raising children. It's fine to disagree or have conflicts with your teenager, but sometimes you can tell that you or your adolescent is getting very angry or frustrated. As the adult, it's your responsibility to know when things are getting too heated and to take appropriate action. You may notice yourself getting angry and raising your voice, or you may notice your teenager getting angry or heated. When this happens try some of the following responses.

Stop and take a time-out from the disagreement, and let things cool down. You can always say, "I want to take some time and think about this before we talk any more." Your teenager may try to keep arguing, but just let it go for now.

Once you call time-out, be patient. Ordering your teenager to "calm down" will rarely get him to calm down; in fact, it may backfire. It may take time for him to accept the time-out.

Remember, strong anger goes away on its own with time. Given time, things will cool down. The disagreement may still be there, and that's normal, but the strong anger will cool down. Nobody stays angry permanently.

Remember, "getting your anger out" often makes things worse, not better. In years past, people thought that it was healthy to let negative feelings out and express their anger toward other people. This approach, however, is often not helpful and can harm your relationship in the long run. People rarely get anything settled by yelling, screaming, name calling, or violence.

Learn When it's Time to Stop

The time to stop is before things have escalated to the point that people are saying or doing things that they will regret. Learn where this point is with your teenager. Learn where this point is with yourself—and stop the discussion before it is too late.

If your teenager calls time-out first, respect that. Come back to the issue later, when things have settled down.

Be Ready to Communicate Openly When You Least Expect It

You can't always predict when your teenager will want to talk to you. It rarely occurs when the parent tries to push it. If you push it, you may get a response of "I don't know," or "Who cares?" At other times, the teen may begin to open up on his own, when you least expect it. The key is to be ready to use good communication skills when these times occur. Making time for positive activities with your teenager can increase the likelihood of your teen communicating with you. For example, going fishing, cooking a meal, or going grocery shopping together provides opportunities for communication.

Give Your Adolescents a Hug Every Day and Tell Them That You Love Them

This is a first step in starting good communication. This will let them know that you support them and care about them.

Talking with Your Adolescent about Sex and Sexuality

While it's important to understand various aspects of your teen's illegal sexual behavior, it's equally important to have good communication with him about sex and sexuality in general. Good information about sexual behavior is important for all teenagers, including those with illegal sexual behavior. Good communication between parents and teens about sex and sexuality—communication that is in line with and supports your values— is equally critical. Studies have shown that most American teenagers learn more about sex and sexuality from peers and from the media than from their parents. Being able to provide good information and to communicate appropriately on sexual topics is helpful to all families, especially those in which sexual behavior has been problematic.

Here are some of the basics about sexual development in children and adolescents. At about 10 years of age, children begin to experience changes in their bodies known as puberty. They grow taller and begin to gain weight, and their sexual organs begin to develop and enlarge. As they enter adolescence, other changes occur, including breast and penis development, menstruation, growth of pubic and facial hair, and changes in hormones. The changes in hormones affect adolescents' sexual interests, thoughts, and behaviors.

Most teens know about sexual intercourse, contraception, and sexually transmitted infections (STIs). However, they often have lots of misinformation, such as thinking that birth control pills will prevent

STIs. Some teens participate in health education programs through their schools. Research has shown that these teens are better informed than those who obtain information from the media or from other adolescents. Participation in sex education programs results in teens

- delaying the onset of sexual intercourse;
- having less frequent sex;
- increasing the use of contraceptives when they become sexually active; and
- having fewer sexual partners.

Studies show that—whether parents like it or not—the majority of U.S. teenagers are engaging in some form of sexual behavior and that the age of first intercourse is getting younger and younger. The rates of sexual activity by teens have increased almost 80 percent in the past 35 years. In 2007, a national survey found that nearly 50 percent of students in grades 9 through 12 reported that they had had sexual intercourse and 15 percent reported having intercourse with four or more partners. The incidence of oral-genital contact is increasing, among pre-adolescents as well as adolescents.

It is clear that it is normal for teens to explore and experiment with sexual behavior, and this can include behaviors with same-sex peers. Although adolescents can describe the risks involved with sexual activity, such as STIs or pregnancy, they rarely think that these problems will affect them. They don't know that about 25 percent of their peers who are sexually active have contracted an STI. Some STIs, such as herpes, have no known cure.

Given your son's or daughter's history of sexually abusive behavior, it is important for you to stress that normal and legal sexual behavior involves activity between peers that is clearly based on consent. "Consent" means that 1) both participants agree to the behavior, 2) force, pressure, or violence are not involved, and 3) the participants are of legal age and capable of giving consent. Many parents are uncomfortable talking with their children about sex. They think that teenagers should not be having sex and that talking about sex gives the wrong message. Some believe that sex should only take place within a marriage. But the reality in our society is that teens are being sexually active in increasing numbers. They are being bombarded with messages about sex and sexuality from their peers and from the media. Given this reality, it is important for parents to discuss sex and sexuality with their children as appropriate to each child's level of understanding and to frame these discussions within their own beliefs and values. It is important that parents help their children acquire accurate information and form healthy values and attitudes about sex.

Controversial Treatment Practices

Some practices currently used in the treatment and supervision of adolescents with illegal sexual behavior are controversial, meaning that experts in the field disagree as to whether they are necessary, appropriate, or effective. These controversial practices include the use of 1) plethysmograph testing (a device placed on a penis to measure arousal); 2) a polygraph (lie detector); 3) sex-offender registries; and 4) community notification.

These practices were all originally designed for and implemented with adult sex offenders to increase the effectiveness of treatment or to provide stronger community safety. Though widely used with adult sex offenders, minimal evidence exists that proves that any of these methods are effective in reducing future sex offenses. No research indicates that these approaches increase treatment effectiveness or community safety when used with adolescents.

Despite this lack of evidence and a growing body of information showing that practices designed for adults can often cause more harm than good with adolescents, these controversial practices continue to be used by some programs as part of the treatment and supervision of adolescents. The concern is that aggressive methods that have not been proven to be effective with adults have "trickled down" to become a standard part of some treatment programs for adolescents. Without clear evidence that they are effective with adolescents, such methods should be used cautiously in a limited number of cases.

Parents should be aware that these methods are controversial. They should discuss with their teen's treatment provider and probation officer which treatment methods will be used.

SEVEN

Reunification

Many adolescents can be safely maintained in their homes during treatment for their offense. Others must be removed from their home in order to provide for the safety of other family members or to provide more intensive treatment. The information below will provide guidelines for making decisions and managing the process of returning the adolescent to the family. The guidelines can apply to all cases but are especially designed for families in which the adolescent was involved with a younger child, such as a sibling or step-sibling, who lives in the home.

Q. Will the adolescent be returned to the family?
A. The adolescent may have been removed from his home by the legal or child protection system or the parents may have decided that it was better for him to live outside the home for a period of time. Many adolescents do return to live with their families. While some things will have changed, such as supervision and rules in the home, those families have been successful in having their family reunified. Whether an adolescent will return to live with his family depends on many factors that include

- the seriousness of the illegal behavior;
- how long the behavior went on;
- the safety of other children in the home;
- the parents' willingness to have the adolescent return home;
- the stability of the family and how well the adolescent will be supervised by the parents;
- the family's participation in the adolescent's treatment program; and
- the adolescents' progress in treatment and successful completion of probation requirements.

Q. How does reunification happen?

A. There are several ways to have an adolescent return to live with his family. Typically the probation officer, CPS worker, treatment provider, and parents will develop a reunification plan to fit the needs of the particular family. The goals are to provide maximum safety for children in the home and to return the adolescent to a more normal setting, i.e., school, friends, activities. While no set list of factors exists that will always lead to a successful reunification, certain guidelines can help in developing and implementing a plan.

Guidelines for Reunification

A set of general guidelines is described below that can be useful in developing a plan for reunifying your teen into the family, i.e., setting a timeline, developing rules for supervision during visitation, and increasing levels of contact between the adolescent and the younger child.

Plans for reunification should first consider the safety and emotional well-being of the victim, if the child is in the home. Listed below are suggestions for an assessment of the parents, the adolescent, and the child victim before the reunification process begins.

Before the reunification process can begin, parents should

- be clear about who was responsible for the abusive behavior;
- be supportive of both the adolescent and the sibling;
- know the details about the behavior, i.e., how and where it happened and all situations that provided opportunities for it to happen;
- recognize warning signs or behaviors and know how to respond;
- participate in the development of a safety plan for the adolescent;
- be able to discuss the behavior with the therapist, the adolescent, and the child; and

- know and be able to enforce the supervision rules in
  the home and community.

Before an adolescent can begin reunification, an assessment needs to be
made to ensure that he is ready for visits and that he has made adequate
progress in treatment. The adolescent needs to

- understand the harm caused to the family, the child,
  and himself;
- be making consistent progress in treatment with
  no major sexual or nonsexual problems at home, at
  school, or in the community;
- have admitted his behavior and taken responsibility
  for it; and
- know and be ready to follow the rules for visitation in
  the home.

In addition, careful consideration needs to be given to how the child
victim is doing before starting reunification. Depending on his or her age
and ability to understand the process, the child victim should

- not have been pressured to begin the process by
  family members who want the adolescent to return
  home;
- be ready for and interested in contact with the
  adolescent;
- have described the behavior in a similar way to what
  the adolescent said happened; and
- be making satisfactory progress or have completed
  treatment, if it was recommended.

The reunification process can begin with the adolescent writing letters
of apology to the victim and his parents as part of his treatment program.
If the victim was a family member who didn't live in the home but was
visiting the family, such as the parents' grandchild, a letter could also be

written to that child's parents. The letter to the adolescent's parents can be read and discussed in a treatment session. If appropriate, the letter to the child victim can be read in a family session prior to or during the reunification process.

A safety plan should be developed by the therapist, the adolescent, the parents, and, when appropriate, the probation officer or CPS worker. The parents should set limits for the adolescent's behavior in the home, know what the adolescent is to do if problematic situations come up, and implement consequences for breaking any of the rules. Some suggestions for a safety plan are listed below. These rules can be adjusted as the adolescent shows that his behavior has changed over time.

During visitation and the reunification process, the adolescent should

- be closely supervised (within the sight of adults who understand the need for supervision) when around children under 12;
- not babysit under any circumstances;
- not be in charge of children under 12 for any activity in such places as a school, church, or rest room;
- not discipline or correct children in the home;
- not go into other children's rooms;
- leave if a child comes into his room;
- not share a room with younger children;
- not be involved in bathing or dressing children;
- be fully dressed when in public areas of the home;
- not have access to highly sexualized materials, including magazines, videos, television shows, or the Internet; and
- not engage in horseplay, wrestling, or tickling with children.

It is important to note that these rules do not mean that an adolescent cannot have ordinary or typical activities for his age with appropriate supervision. He should go to school, church, the mall, or restaurants with family members and be involved in age-appropriate activities that are supervised by adults such as sports activities, band, or other school events. Over time, the adolescent can be allowed to have activities that do not require close supervision as he shows that he can conduct himself in an acceptable way.

The process of reunification can take place in steps such as the ones listed below. The process should be planned with the therapist, probation officer, CPS worker (if one is involved), parents, and the adolescent. While the steps below may not be necessary or appropriate in every case, they can serve as a guideline for planning the reunification process. The steps can be implemented on a weekly basis or on a schedule that is planned by the group involved in developing the safety plan. The length of time to implement the plan should be decided on a case-by-case basis and can last from a few weeks to several months, depending on the circumstances and the successful completion of each step.

Suggested steps for reunification are as follows:

- Letters of apology written
- Assessment of readiness of the adolescent, the child, and the family
- Development of a safety plan
- Phone calls between the adolescent and the child, monitored by the parent or therapist
- Family sessions with the child present, if needed
- Supervised visits out of the home, in a park, restaurant, or another family member's home, with the child present
- Supervised visits in the home for two to four hours
- Supervised all-day visits in the home
- Supervised two-day visits in the home
- Overnight visits in the home
- Weekend visits with overnights
- Extended visits, such as during a holiday period or spring break
- Adolescent returns home

It is strongly recommended that the reunification process be done while the adolescent is in treatment and, if he is on probation, before the probation period ends. This timing will provide the necessary professional involvement, assistance, and oversight to give the process the best chance of being successful.

Q. When should reunification not be considered?
A. The following factors are potential indicators that the adolescent, child victim, or family is not at a point where the reunification process should be implemented. These factors should not be taken as definite reasons not to discuss reunification, but they can help you decide the overall readiness of your family to begin the process.

Reunification should not be considered when

- the abuse was extremely harmful to the child victim;
- the child has significant discomfort when discussing the topic; it is expected, however, that a child might have some uncertainty about discussing the issue;
- the child continues to have significant trauma symptoms or serious response to the abuse;
- evidence exists that the victim has been pressured to agree to reunification; and/or
- the adolescent has a recent history of significant aggressive or violent behavior.

Not all of the above factors taken alone would automatically stop the reunification process; however, each of them should be given careful consideration before starting the process or if they occur as the process is implemented. Other factors may need to be considered, but these will depend on the specifics of each individual case.

EIGHT

Preventing Future Illegal Sexual Behavior

Signs of Problematic Sexual Behavior

Understanding possible signs of problematic sexual behavior is an important part of helping your teen develop safe and healthy behaviors and of protecting younger children in your home. It's important to be aware of behaviors that might signal a return to illegal sexual behavior or a desire to return to illegal sexual behavior. It should be emphasized that none of these behaviors predicts that a teen will commit an illegal sexual behavior. None of these behaviors means that a teen has already committed such a behavior. These behaviors do signal, however, that a problem might exist. Behaviors to be aware of include

- repeatedly breaking the rules during visitation and reunification;
- a high level of interest in or possession of pornography;
- highly aggressive behavior toward younger children;
- the spending of large amounts of time with younger children rather than with adolescents his own age;
- arranging to be alone with young children for extended periods of time; and
- bribing young children to commit other types of inappropriate or illegal behaviors.

What do you do if you see signs of problematic sexual behavior? An adolescent will occasionally break a visitation and reunification rule, but, after being reminded, will be more careful about his behavior. If the adolescent continues to break the rules, however, the parents should increase their supervision and contact the adolescent's therapist and probation officer. An alternative plan may need to be put into place that provides a more secure placement.

NINE

Taking Action

We have tried to discuss the issues and problems that will come up for you, your teen, and your family. Other problems may come up while your son or daughter is in treatment. Be sure to discuss these with your child's treatment provider. It is important that the provider have all of the information that can help your adolescent successfully complete treatment.

Based on our experiences, we can tell you that there is hope for you and your family. Most adolescents complete treatment and do very well as they finish high school and go into young adulthood. We wish you and your family the very best as you take action to support your adolescent.

RESOURCES

Web Resources

4Parents.gov
  Government site for parents with tips for talking to children, preteens, and teens about healthy and safe sexual behavior choices.

MVParents.com
  Research-based resource with tips, ideas, and strategies for raising smart, strong, responsible kids.

National Center for Sexual Behavior of Youth
www.NCSBY.org
  Information about children with sexual behavior problems and adolescents with illegal sexual behavior.

Books for Parents and Youth

Gravelle, K., and J. Gravelle. 1996. *The Period Book: Everything You Don't Want to Ask (But Need to Know)*. New York: Walker and Company.

Hafner, D. W. 1999. *From Diapers to Dating: A Parent's Guide to Raising Sexually Healthy Children*. New York: Newmarket Press.

Harris, R. H., and M. Emberly. 1996. *It's Perfectly Normal: Changing Bodies, Growing Up, Sex, and Sexual Health*. Cambridge, MA: Candlewick Press.

Herrerias, C. 1996. *Teen to Teen: Personal Safety and Sexual Abuse Prevention*. Charlotte, NC: Kidsrights, Inc.

Johnson, T. C. 1999. *Understanding Your Child's Sexual Behavior: What's Natural and Healthy*. Oakland, CA: New Harbinger Publications.

Jones, M. 2007. "The Case of the Juvenile Sex Offender." *New York Times Magazine*, July 22:33–39, 56–59.

Madaras, L. 2003. *Ready, Set, Grow*. New York: Newmarket Press.

Madaras, L., and A. Madaras. 2000. *The What's Happening to My Body? Book for Boys: A Growing-Up Guide for Parents and Sons*. New York: Newmarket Press.

Mayle, P. 1973. *Where Did I Come From?*. Seacacus, NJ: Lyle Stuart, Inc.

———. 1975. *What's Happening to Me?* Seacacus, NJ: Lyle Stuart, Inc.

Schaefer, V., and N. Bendell. 1998. *The Care and Keeping of You: The Body Book for Girls*. Middleton, WI: Pleasant Company Publications.

Stoppard, M. 1997. *Sex Ed: Growing Up, Relationships, and Sex*. New York: DK Publishing.

BARBARA L. BONNER, Ph.D., is a clinical child psychologist, professor of pediatrics at the University of Oklahoma, and the Children's Medical Research Institutes's Jean Gumerson Endowed Chair recipient. She is the director of the Center on Child Abuse and Neglect and the associate director of the Child Study Center. Dr. Bonner has won numerous awards for her work with children and advocacy for children. She has served as president of the American Professional Society on the Abuse of Children (APSAC) and of the International Society on the Prevention of Child Abuse and Neglect (ISPCAN), and has been invited to speak nationally and internationally on her work with children and adolescents with problematic sexual behavior.